Splash!

By Joy Cowley

Illustrated by Jane Molineaux

Dominie Press, Inc.

Publisher: Christine Yuen
Editor: John S. F. Graham
Designer: Lois Stanfield
Illustrator: Jane Molineaux

Published by:

🐘 **Dominie Press, Inc.**

1949 Kellogg Avenue
Carlsbad, California 92008 USA

www.dominie.com

Paperback ISBN 0-7685-1066-X
Library Bound Edition ISBN 0-7685-1499-1
Printed in Singapore by PH Productions Pte Ltd
   2 3 4 5 6 PH 04 03

Table of Contents

Chapter One
We Need Water

The three little pigs
wanted to clean their windows.

"We need water," said Patrick Pig.

"From the river," said Polly Pig.

"In a bucket," said Peter Pig.
"I will go and get it."
So Peter Pig went—
tritty-trot, tritty-trot, tritty-trot
down to the big, deep river.

He stopped on the river bank
and lifted his bucket.

5

Whammo!

Out of the bushes
jumped Mr. B. B. Wolf.

"Peter Pig, Peter Pig!
What are you doing here?"

"I've come to get some water,"
said Peter Pig in a small voice.

"Forget it!" said Mr. B. B. Wolf.

Chapter Two
A Riddle

Mr. B. B. Wolf smiled
a nasty smile.

"I am going to ask you a riddle,"
he said.

"If you can't tell me the answer,
I'll toss you into the river."

Peter Pig shivered
down to his trotters.

"This is the riddle,"
said Mr. B. B. Wolf.
"Do you see what I see?
Do you hear what I hear?
Do you know what I know?"

Peter Pig said in his small voice,
"How can I see what you see?
How can I hear what you hear?
How can I know what you know?
I'm not you!"

"That's not the answer!"
bellowed Mr. B. B. Wolf.
"Into the river you go!"

Splash!

Chapter Three

I Don't Know
What You Know

Polly Pig looked
down the path.
"Peter is taking a long time
to get that water,"
she said to her brother Patrick.
"I'll go and look for him."

So off went Polly Pig—
tritty-trot, tritty-trot, tritty-trot
on the path to the big, deep river.

Whammo!

Out jumped Mr. B. B. Wolf.

"Polly Pig! Polly Pig!" he bellowed.
"What are you doing here?"

"I'm looking for my brother Peter,"
said Polly Pig
in a small, squeaky voice.

"He's in the river!"
said Mr. B. B. Wolf.
"You'll go into the river, too,
if you don't answer my riddle."

Polly Pig shook and shivered.

"Do you see what I see?"
said the wolf with a nasty smile.
"Do you hear what I hear?
Do you know what I know?"

In her small, squeaky voice,
Polly Pig said,
"I don't see what you see.
I don't hear what you hear.
I don't know what you know."

"Then into the river you go!"
shouted Mr. B. B. Wolf.

Splash!

Chapter Four

A Very Nasty Wolf

Patrick Pig frowned
as he looked down the path.
"First Peter, and now Polly," he said.
"What's the bet they've met
that horrible, nasty bully,
Mr. B. B. Wolf?
I will go and rescue them."

With that,
Patrick Pig went—
tritty-trot, tritty-trot, tritty-trot
to the bank of the river.
All he saw was a plastic bucket.

"Peter!" he called. "Polly!"

Whammo!

Mr. B. B. Wolf jumped out of
the bushes.

"I tossed them into the river because
they couldn't answer my riddle,"
Mr. B. B. Wolf said.
"See if you can do better, Patrick Pig.
This is the riddle:
Do you see what I see?
Do you hear what I hear?
Do you know what I know?"

Patrick Pig shook his head.
"You are a very nasty wolf,
and that is a very stupid riddle,"
he said.

Splash!

Chapter Five

Mrs. Cow

The three little pigs ran home—
tritty-trot, tritty-trot, tritty-trot.
They were very wet and cold.

Mrs. Cow stared at them.

"Where have you been?" she said.

"The river," said Peter Pig.

"The big, deep river," said Polly Pig.

"Tossed in by that horrible,
nasty bully, Mr. B. B. Wolf,"
said Patrick Pig.

"Well, bless my moo!
What a thing to do!"
said Mrs. Cow, rolling her eyes.
"But you mustn't call him names.
I'm sure he didn't mean to be bad.
Maybe he was lonely.
Maybe he was sad."

The pigs looked at each other.

Mrs. Cow said,
"You must give him a chance
to say that he is sorry."

Chapter Six

Whammo!

Tritty-trot, tritty-trot, tritty-trot.
The three little pigs
went back to the river
to see Mr. B. B. Wolf.

"You again!" snarled the wolf.
"Wasn't one swim enough?"

The pigs shook in their trotters,
but they tried to be brave.

"We think you didn't mean
to be a bully," said Peter Pig.

"We think maybe you were lonely,"
said Polly Pig.

"Or maybe you were sad,"
said Patrick Pig.

Mr. B. B. Wolf
smiled his nasty smile.
"Into the river you all go!" he bellowed.

Whammo!

Mrs. Cow jumped out of the bushes.
"Wait a minute!" she said to the wolf.

Chapter Seven

From Nose to Tail

Mrs. Cow's smile
was as sweet
as buttercups and daisies.
She said to Mr. B. B. Wolf,
"I have a riddle for you.
Do you see what I see?
Do you hear what I hear?
Do you know what I know?"

Mr. B. B. Wolf looked at Mrs. Cow.
Mrs. Cow was very big,
and she had long, sharp horns.
He began to shiver
from nose to tail.

He said in a whisper,
"You see a shivering wolf.
You hear his chattering teeth.
You know that you are going
to toss him into that water."

"Very good," said Mrs. Cow.

"Why don't I save you the trouble?"
said Mr. B. B. Wolf.
"Why don't I toss myself
into the big, deep river?"

"Very good again," said Mrs. Cow.

Splash!

Chapter Eight

Bullies Never Do Well

The three little pigs
looked out of their clean windows.
Mr. B. B. Wolf was slinking past—
slippitty-slop, slippitty slop.

He was very wet and cold.

"Would you like a dry towel?"
called Peter Pig.

"Or some hot soup?"
said Polly Pig.

31

"Or a warm jacket?"
said Patrick Pig.

The wolf scowled and growled.
"Get lost!" he cried
as he slipped and dripped
past their window.

The three little pigs
sat down at their table
to eat hot soup and corn bread.
"Bullies never do well,"
said Patrick Pig
with a happy sigh.